Animals in the Wild

Panda

by Mary Hoffman

Windward/Belitha Press

Panda cubs are born tiny. This one was only a day
old and weighed only 60 grams. She was one of two
cubs born in Madrid Zoo in Spain. For the first
four days the cub clings tightly to its mother.
After six weeks its eyes open, and it can hear.
It is four months before it can crawl on its own.

This cub is six months old, weighs about 12 kilos and has a black and white fur coat. His name is Towi which means "little boy". He lives with his mother Ying in a zoo in Mexico. Pandas in zoos don't often have babies so cubs like these two are very special. Their natural home is far away.

Giant pandas live in the high bamboo forests of China. This one is among its favourite food.

They are shy of humans and keep out of their way.
There are not many giant pandas left in the wild.

The Chinese had always known about the panda but
no one outside China knew that in these misty and
mysterious forests lived a black and white giant.
Then foreign hunters came and sometimes killed them.

When people realized how special pandas were, they started to bring them back alive for other people to see. It wasn't until 50 years ago that a live panda was first seen in a zoo outside China.

In the wild, the giant panda spends most
of its time moving slowly along the ground.
But it is also a good climber and can

get up trees very quickly. It does this when
it is frightened or when it wants a quiet sleep
in the branches. Even in a zoo it climbs trees.

Because the giant panda comes from a wet and rainy part of the world, it likes water. Some pandas like swimming. The ones that are kept in zoos are usually given a pool to play in. They also like water-sprays and blocks of ice. When they are young, pandas are very playful.

That's one reason why they have become one of
the most popular animals ever shown in zoos.
Since the giant panda was brought to America
and England in the nineteen-thirties, almost
every big zoo in the West has wanted to have one.
People will always come to see a panda playing.

Zoos now do a good job helping pandas to survive.
The giant panda eats a lot of bamboo. In the wild
it needs about twenty kilos a day. It grips the
tough bamboo stem using the claws and a bony knob

in its paw, while it strips the leaves off with
its massive teeth. But bamboos sometimes die
before producing new plants, and giant pandas in
the wild can die for lack of this basic food.

You can easily spot the giant panda with its large
white face, its black eye patches and round black
ears. Its legs are black too and it has a band
of black fur around its chest. When adult it grows
to weigh over a hundred kilos. Standing on its
four paws it is about fifty centimetres high.

The markings are quite clear on this young panda,
walking slowly on all fours. Most of the panda's
fur is white, and the Chinese name for it means
"white bear". But zoologists don't all agree
that pandas are related to bears. Some think
they are closer to the raccoons.

This doesn't seem so strange if you look at the other kind of panda. The red panda is much smaller than its giant relative, with beautiful chestnut coloured stripes on its tail.

It has the same kind of paw as the giant panda and uses it in the same way to grasp its favourite food, bamboo. The red panda eats a wider range of foods than the giant, and is less dependent on bamboo.

It comes from the mountain forests of South-East
Asia and from West China, where the bamboo grows.
The red panda is a beautiful animal but isn't as
well known as the giant black and white panda.

Zoos do what they can to look after their pandas
and to help them produce cubs. The Chinese are
trying hard to help them find enough food. All
pandas need help from people in order to survive.

First published 1983 by Windward

An imprint owned by
W. H. Smith & Son Limited
Registered No. 237811 England
Trading as WHS Distributors, St. John's House,
East Street, Leicester LE1 6NE

by arrangement with Belitha Press Ltd
40 Belitha Villas, London N1 1PD

Dedicated to Sara

Scientific Adviser: Dr Gwynne Vevers
Picture Researcher: Stella Martin
Designer: Julian Holland

Acknowledgements are due to Bruce Coleman Ltd for all
photographs in this book with the following exceptions:
Sergio Dorantes pp 12–13, 19, 23; Jacana Ltd Front cover,
pp 1, 8, 9, 10; John Knight p 2; Stella Martin Back cover,
pp 11, 14; Rex Features Ltd pp 3, 7.

Printed by W. S. Cowell Ltd
8 Butter Market, Ipswich, Suffolk